The Weather
SNOW

Terry Jennings

Chrysalis Education

Distributed in the United States by
Smart Apple Media
2140 Howard Drive West
North Mankato, Minnesota 56003

Library of Congress Control Number: 2003070062

ISBN 1-59389-145-8

Produced by Bender Richardson White, U.K.

Editorial Manager: Joyce Bentley
Project Editors: Lionel Bender and Clare Lewis
Designer: Ben White
Production: Kim Richardson
Picture Researcher: Cathy Stastny
Cover Make-up: Mike Pilley, Radius

Printed in China

10 9 8 7 6 5 4 3 2 1

Words in **bold** can be found in New words on page 31.

Picture credits and copyrights
Corbis Images Inc.: pages 23, 25 (Galen Rowell). Digital Vision Inc.: page 4. Ecoscene: pages 6 (Papilio/Robert Pickett), 9 (Sally Morgan), 11 (Chinch Gryniewicz), 13 (Jim Winkley), 15 (Andrew Brown), 16 (Robin Redfern), 21 (Fritz Polking), 22 (Fritz Polking), 27 (Stuart Donachie). Natural History Photo Agency: page 17 (Laurie Campbell). PhotoDisc Inc.: pages 1 (Neil Beer), 2 (Neil Beer), 18 (Glen Allison), 20 (Sami Sarkis). Rex Features Ltd.: pages 5 (Sipa), 7 (Ray Tang), 12 (David Graves), 14 (Chris Martin Bahr). Steve Gorton: pages 26, 29. Stockholm Tourism: page 28. Terry Jennings: page 24. Weatherstock: cover and pages 8, 10, 19.

Contents

What is snow?

Snow is **frozen** rain. Often, in very cold weather, tiny drops of water in **clouds** become frozen.

The raindrops turn into flakes of **ice** and fall to the ground.

Snowflakes

If you look at **snowflakes** with a magnifying glass, you see beautiful shapes. All snowflakes have six points.

When it is snowing, millions upon millions of snowflakes fall from the sky.

Footprints in snow

New snow is soft. As you walk on snow, your feet sink into it and make footprints.

Animals also leave footprints in the snow. These pawprints were made by a rabbit.

Snowdrifts

Sometimes the wind blows the snow into large heaps called **snowdrifts**. These can block roads and railroads.

Snowplows are used to clear the snow from the roads and railroads.

Blizzards

If the wind blows hard while it is snowing, we say there is a **blizzard**.

The roads are dangerous in a blizzard. They are slippery and drivers cannot easily see people or other cars and trucks.

Plants and snow

Snow is cold. It also stops sunlight reaching the leaves of plants. If snow falls on plants, it can kill them.

Some plants, like snowdrops, are not harmed by snow. They grow up through the snow.

Mountain snow

It can be very cold at the top of high mountains. These are always covered with snow, even in the summer.

Some plants, like snowdrops, are not harmed by snow. They grow up through the snow.

Animals and snow

It is hard for many animals to find food in the snow. A dormouse sleeps through the winter to avoid the snow.

A European robin does not mind the snow and comes to gardens for food. Its feathers keep its body warm.

Mountain snow

It can be very cold at the top of high mountains. These are always covered with snow, even in the summer.

In the winter, the snow on mountains is often very deep.

At the Poles

The **North Pole** and the **South Pole** are always very cold.

There is always snow and ice on the ground, even in summer. The seas nearby are often frozen solid.

Polar animals

Many animals that live near the North Pole and the South Pole have layers of **waterproof** feathers or thick, white **fur**.

The fur keeps them warm. The white color makes it hard for their enemies to see them.

Living with snow

Near the North Pole, houses are built with steep sloping roofs so the snow falls off quickly as it **melts**.

The people often wear
clothes made of fur to
keep them warm.

Moving on snow

It is difficult to move on snow. People wear skis, **snowshoes**, or big boots to stop them sinking.

A **snowmobile** does not have wheels. It slides across the snow.

Fun in the snow

It is fun to ski in the snow, or skate on ice. Make sure you keep warm.

You need warm clothes when
you play in the snow.

Quiz

1 When does it usually snow?

2 What do we leave behind if we walk in the snow?

3 What are the heaps of snow blown by the wind called?

4 What color are many of the animals
near the North and South Poles?

5 Is there snow in summer on the tops of very
high mountains?

6 What do some animals, like the dormouse, do in winter?

7 Does a snowmobile have wheels?

8 What kind of clothes should you wear
in the snow?

The answers are all in this book!

New words

blizzard a windy snowstorm.

cloud a mass of tiny water drops.

frozen to be changed into ice by cold; feeling very cold.

fur the soft hair on an animal's body.

ice frozen water.

melt to change something into a liquid, for example, turning snow or ice to water by warming it.

North Pole the top end of the earth; at the center of a huge area of snow and ice called the Arctic.

South Pole the bottom end of the earth; at the center of a huge area of snow and ice called the Antarctic.

snowdrift snow blown by wind into a big heap or mound.

snowflake a little piece of ice that falls from clouds.

snowmobile a machine, like a scooter, for riding on snow and ice.

snowplow a machine for clearing snow from roads and railroads.

snowshoe a large, flat shoe used for walking over snow.

waterproof keeps out water so things, animals, plants, or people stay dry.

Index